ZEN SMILES

BY
RAHUL KARN

DEDICATED TO
ALL THE
MEDITATORS
OF
PAST,
PRESENT
& FUTURE

PREFACE

Dear Zen Friends,

Thanks for welcoming the Zensational Stories series.
Though I kept on eliciting your hidden psychology and hurting your religious sentiments, you kept on smiling. So, I thought to come up with a book having collections of those Zen Stories which will make you smile.
Buddha never cracked any joke. But Zen Masters keep on creating humorous situations. Sometimes they look crazy too. But looking crazy is better than being a serious man who never smiles. So, I think the book is very relevant is modern context where people have become very serious in the pursuit of achieving their goals. These stories are very old and have been taken from various old records. But the smile they continue to bring on people's face is always fresh like dewdrops.
There is another specialty of this work. Unlike other volumes, I have not written any commentary on the stories, because the sound of raindrops does not need any commentary. Thus, this book is equally useful for new as well as old students of Zen!
Should you have any queries, please feel free to mail me on zensationalstories@gmail.com.
Have a Zensational time!

Yours Zen Friend
Rahul Karn
Melbourne
20th March 2017

CONTENTS

- PREFACE _____ 3
- 1. The Fundamental Idea _____ 7
- 2. The Found Money _____ 8
- 3. Rainy and Sunny Days _____ 9
- 4. A Formal Discourse _____ 10
- 5. Big Belly Laugh _____ 11
- 6. Let It Be _____ 12
- 7. Nostrils _____ 13
- 8. The Meaning _____ 14
- 9. The Laughing Person _____ 15
- 10. No Zen Teachers _____ 16
- 11. Precious _____ 17
- 12. The Green Color _____ 18
- 13. The Woman at The Inn _____ 20
- 14. Flavors of Life _____ 22
- 15. The Hearty Laugh _____ 23
- 16. Hell _____ 24
- 17. A Pile of Dry Shit _____ 25
- 18. Angry Buddha _____ 26
- 19. Solution _____ 28
- 20. Everything Is Still There _____ 30
- 21. The Master's Smile _____ 32
- 22. Doubt _____ 33
- 23. Solution _____ 34

24.	Any Question	35
25.	Sign	36
26.	Miracle	37
27.	The Last Rap	38
28.	Who Are Buddhas?	39
29.	Half Approve, Half Not Approve	40
30.	The Complete Entrance	41
31.	Donkey	42
32.	Illness	43
33.	The Question	44
34.	Perception	45
35.	Tradition	46
36.	The Buddha In The Home	47
37.	Monkey's Response	48
38.	Understanding	49
39.	Archery	50
40.	People	51
41.	The Painting	52
42.	Let Go	54
43.	Emotion	55
44.	The Mind	56
45.	The True Self	57
46.	Imitation	58
47.	The Strange Advice	59
48.	Fees	60
49.	Correct	61

50.	**The Entrance To Zen**	62
	What Next?	63
	Bibliography	64

1. The Fundamental Idea

Someone asked: "What is the fundamental idea of Zen?"

Zen Master Yun-men: "When spring comes, the grass turns green of itself."

2. The Found Money

Once upon a time, there was a poor man who picked up a sack of money in the streets. He was overwhelmed with happiness. Then he began to count the money. Suddenly, the real owner of the money showed up. He had to give back the whole sack. He regretted for not having gone off to a faraway place sooner. He felt great pain for his loss.

3. Rainy and Sunny Days

An old woman cried everyday under the tree. People did not know why.

One day, a monk passed by and asked her why she cried so sadly. The old woman said, "I have two daughters, the elder selling umbrella and the younger selling dried food. On sunny days, I cry because my elder daughter cannot make a living as nobody buys umbrellas. On rainy days, I cry because my younger daughter cannot make or sell dried food."

The monk then told the old woman, "I can make you happy! Oh dear, you should think of your elder daughter on rainy days. You will be happy because people buy umbrellas from her. On sunny days, you should think of your younger daughter because she can earn a lot of money by selling dried food."

The old woman was suddenly enlightened. Since then, she laughed everyday under the tree.

4. A Formal Discourse

One day Zen Master Yang-Chi (992-1049) got up to address a group seeking enlightenment and had only this to say:

"Ha! Ha! Ha! What's all this? Go to the back of the hall and have some tea!"

He then got down and departed!!!

5. Big Belly Laugh

Of the great Zen Master Rinzai, it was said that each night the last thing he did before he went to bed was let out a great big belly laugh that resounded through the corridors and was heard in every building of the monastery grounds. And the first thing he did when he woke at dawn was burst into peals of laughter so loud they woke up every monk no matter how deep his slumber. His disciples asked him repeatedly to tell them why he laughed but he wouldn't. And when he died he carried the secret of his laughter with him to the grave.

6. Let It Be

Before Ch'an (Chinese: Ch'an, Japanese: Zen) Master Pao-fu passed away he told his disciples, "I have been feeling weak lately. I suspect that it is almost time for me to go."

Upon hearing this, some of his disciples said, "Master, you still look very healthy."

Others implored, "Master, we still need your guidance," while some urged, "Master, please stay for the sake of all beings."

One disciple asked, "Master, when it is time for you to go, will you go or will you stay?"

Master Pao-fu asked, "which do you think would be better?"

The disciple answered without hesitation, "Whether it is life or death, let it be!"

The Master started laughing, "When did you steal the words that I was going to use?"

Upon saying this, Pao-fu passed away.

7. Nostrils

A monk asked, "Where are one's nostrils before one is born?"

Zen Master Nansen replied, "Where are one's nostrils after one has been born?"

8. The Meaning

Someone asked, "What is the meaning of Bodhidharma's coming from the West?"
[This is a very famous Zen question which means what is the ultimate truth?]
The Zen Patriarch Ma-Tsu hit him, and said, "If I don't hit you, people everywhere will laugh at me."

9. The Laughing Person

Great Master Yuanming of Deshan instructed his assembly and said, "If you have exhausted to the end, you will realize right way that all Buddhas in the three worlds (that is of past, present and future) have stuck their mouths to the wall (that is they are unable to speak). Yet there is still one person – he is giving a great laugh. If you can recognize that person, you have accomplished your study!"

10. No Zen Teachers

When Zen Master Huang Po had taken his place in the assembly hall, he began:

"You people are just like drunkards. I don't know how you manage to keep on your feet in such a sodden condition. Why, everyone will die laughing at you. It all seems so easy, so why do we have to live to see a day like this? Can't you understand that in the whole Empire of the T'ang there are no 'teachers of Zen'?"

A monk stepped forth and asked, "How can you say that? At this very moment, as all can see, we are sitting face to face with one who has appeared in the world to be a teacher of monks and a leader of men (that is you)!"

"Please note that I did not say there is no Zen," answered the Master, "I merely pointed out that there are no TEACHERS!"

11. Precious

A wise woman who was traveling in the mountains found a precious stone in a stream. The next day she met another traveler who was hungry, and the wise woman opened her bag to share her food.

The hungry traveler saw the precious stone and asked the woman to give it to him. She did so without hesitation. The traveler left, rejoicing in his good fortune. He knew the stone was worth enough to give him security for a lifetime. But a few days later he came back to return the stone to the wise woman.

"I've been thinking," he said, "I know how valuable the stone is, but I give it back in the hope that you can give me something even more precious. Please share with me what you have within you that enabled you to give me the stone without hesitation."

The wise woman laughed. "Young man, there is nothing more for me to share with you. By returning the stone you have shown that you already have what is most precious, within yourself as well."

12. The Green Color

There was a millionaire who was bothered by severe eye pain. He consulted so many physicians and was getting his treatment done. He did not stop consulting galaxy of medical experts; he consumed heavy loads of drugs and underwent hundreds of injections.

But the ache persisted with great vigor than before. At last a monk who has supposed to be an expert in treating such patients was called for by the millionaire. The monk understood his problem and said that for some time he should concentrate only on green colors and not to fall his eyes on any other colors.

The millionaire got together a group of painters and purchased barrels of green color and directed that every object his eye was likely to fall to be painted in green color just as the monk had directed.

When the monk came to visit him after few days, the millionaire's servants ran with buckets of green paints and poured on him since he was in red dress, lest their master not see any other color and his eye ache would come back.

Hearing this monk laughed said "If only you had purchased a pair of green spectacles, worth just a few rupees, you could have saved these walls and trees and pots and all other articles and also could have saved a large share of his fortune. You cannot paint the world green."

13. The Woman at The Inn

There was a woman who kept the pilgrim's inn at Hara under Mount Fuji. Her name is unknown, and it is not known when she was born or died.

She went to hear a talk by Hakuin who said, "They say there's a pure land where everything is only mind, and that there's a Buddha of light in your own body. Once that Buddha of light appears, mountains, rivers, earth, grass, trees, and forests suddenly glow with a great light. To see this, you have to look inside your own heart. Then what should you be looking out for? When you are looking for something that is only mind, what kind of special features would it have? When you are looking for the Buddha of infinite light in your own body, how would you recognize it?"

When she heard this, the woman said, "This isn't so hard." Back at home she meditated day and night, holding the question while she was awake and during her sleep. One day, as she was washing a pot, she had a sudden breakthrough. She threw the pot aside and rushed to see Hakuin.

She said, "I've met Buddha in my own body, and everything on earth is shining with a great light! It's wonderful!" She danced for joy.

"Is that so?" said Hakuin, "but what about a pit of shit, does it also shine with a great light?"

The woman ran up and slapped him. She said, "You still don't get it, you old fart!"

Hakuin roared with laughter.

14. Flavors of Life

In the early autumn of 1925, Master Hongyi was left stranded by war at Qita Temple in the city of Ningbo. One day, his old friend Xia Mianzun paid him a visit. Seeing that there was only one dish of salted vegetable on the table, Xia could not help but ask, "Isn't it too salty?"

"Salty as it is, it has its own taste," said Master Hongyi.

After the meal, Master Hongyi poured himself a cup of plain water.

Xia asked again, "Isn't there any tea? Why do you drink that tasteless water?"

Master Hongyi laughed and said, "Tasteless as it is, it has its own taste too."

15. The Hearty Laugh

The great Zen Master Weiyan of Yaoshan, like many well-known Zen Masters, came to be identified by his place of residence, and so he was called Yaoshan. One evening, Yaoshan went for a walk in the hills. Suddenly, the clouds and fog parted, and the moon could be seen shining brightly in the sky. On seeing this, Yaoshan let out a hearty laugh. It was so loud that it could be heard for miles in all directions.

16. Hell

One day Zen master Kyong Ho went for a walk in the country with the young student, Yong Song Sunim, who was known for his kindness. They came to a standby the road where a group of boys had dozens and dozens of frogs on a string, and were selling them.

Yong Song implored his teacher to take a rest, and then went back to the boys and bought all of the frogs and set them free. After the last of the frogs hop the way, Yong Song smiled to himself and went to his master and said, "How fortunate that we came this way. I just saved all those frogs!"

"That is wonderful," said Kyong Ho, "but you're going straight to hell."

"What?" Yong Song was startled to hear this. "I've read the frogs. Why should I go to Hell?"

"You already understand."

"No, I don't. Please teach me," begged Yong Song.

"You say 'I' save for those frogs. But this 'I' doesn't exist. Making this 'I' is a big mistake. Keep that 'I-me' mind, and you're going to hell like an arrow."

17. A Pile of Dry Shit

One day a famous government officer met a highly respected elderly master. Being conceited, he wanted to prove that he was the superior person.

As their conversation drew on, he asked the master, "Old monk, do you know what I think of you and the things you said?"

The master replied, "I don't care what you think of me. You are entitled to have your own opinion."

The officer snorted, "Well, I will tell you what I think anyway. In my eyes, you are just like a pile of dry shit!"

The master simply smiled and stayed quiet.

Seeing that his insult had fallen into deaf ears, he asked curiously, "And what do you think of me?"

The master said, "In my eyes, you are just like the Buddha."

Hearing this remark, the officer left happily and bragged to his wife about the incident.

His wife said to him, "You conceited fool! When a person has a heart like a pile of dry shit, he sees everyone in that light. The elderly master has a heart like that of the Buddha, and that is why in his eyes, everyone, including you, is like the Buddha!"

18. Angry Buddha

A woman who practices reciting Buddha Amitabha's name, is very tough and recites "NAMO AMITABHA BUDDHA" three times daily. Although she is doing this practice for over 10 years, she is still quite mean, shouting at people all the time. She starts her practice lighting incense and hitting a little bell.

A friend wanted to teach her a lesson, and just as she began her recitation, he came to her door and called out: "Miss Nuyen, Miss Nuyen!".

As this was the time for her practice she got annoyed, but she said to herself: "I have to struggle against my anger, so I will just ignore it." And she continued: "NAMO AMITABHA BUDDHA, NAMO AMITABHA BUDDHA..."

But the man continued to shout her name, and she became more and more oppressive.

She struggled against it and wondered if she should stop the recitation to give the man a piece of her mind, but she continued reciting: "NAMO AMITABHA BUDDHA, NAMO AMITABHA BUDDHA..."

The man outside heard it and continued: "Miss Nuyen, Miss Nuyen..."

Then she could not stand it anymore, jumped up, slammed the door and went to the gate and shouted: "Why do you have to behave like that? I am doing my practice and you keep on shouting my name over and over!"

The gentleman smiled at her and said: "I just called your name for ten minutes and you are so angry. You have been calling Amitabha Buddha's name for more than ten years now; just imagine how angry he must be by now!"

19. Solution

Once there was a saint in a village. Nearby was a man living in great poverty. He had a family with 5 members. He had 3 goats, 2 cows, 2 buffalos and one dog. His cottage was so small. He frequently visited the saint and asked for his remedies to overcome the striking poverty.

Saint told him to put the dog inside his cottage daily and meet him after a week. Dog should never go out. That man agreed.

Next week he met the saint. How do you do now, asked the saint.

He told that his suffering got increased mildly.

After a brief thinking saint ordered him to keep the 2 cows inside his cottage. They should never go out. He should meet him after a week.

Next week, this man went to the saint. Started complaining, "I am suffering more now. Not able to withstand. Things are becoming worst now."

Within no time saint told him, "Now, you tie those 2 buffalos also inside your house. We will meet next week."

In next week, this man ran to the saint and cried loudly, "I am unable to understand why I get such a miserable position even after meeting you and greeting you."

Smilingly said the saint, "only few weeks, my son. Now you tie up your 3 goats inside the house" and he got to his feet" don't forget to meet me next week by this time."

Next week this man gone to the saint and told, "Now I am finished. I have not breathed for one week since we met last."

Saint told him to get the dog out of his cottage and meet him next week.

Next week he met the saint with some happiness," I feel some improvement now.'

Said the saint'" Ok, my son. Now you can keep the 2 buffalos outside your cottage. Meet me after the third day."

On third day, this man met the saint in a relaxed condition. He could smile back occasionally.

"Still better now" said he.

Saint immediately told, "I can make you still happier now. Keep the 2 cows out side from today and meet me after 2 days."

He did so.

Now saint said," Ok my son. Now I am going to set you completely free. Keep those 3 goats outside from now on. Meet me tomorrow morning"

Next day this man went to the saint and worshipped him. "Thank you. I got relieved of my problems now"

And that is Zen!

20. Everything Is Still There

A Zen monk Ikkyū had been meditating alone for quite a few days without uttering a word. His master saw him through and then brought him outside of the temple with a smile.

Outside the temple beautiful spring scenery was to be enjoyed – fresh air, peak green shoots of grass, birds darting through the air, and murmuring brooks.

Ikkyū took a deep breath and then peeked at his master. The master was composedly sitting at the hillside for Zen meditation.

A bit confused, Ikkyū had no idea of what the master was up to.

As the afternoon was passed, the master stood up and motioned Ikkyū back to the temple.

As soon as the master entered the door of the temple, he suddenly turned around and shut the double wood doors gently, leaving Ikkyū outside.

Not knowing what the master's intention, Ikkyū just sat outside alone to ponder on the master's motivation.

Very soon it got dark and the mist clouded the surrounding hills. The woods, the brooks, and the sound of birds and waves could be seen or heard no more.

At that moment, the master called Ikkyū from inside. Ikkyū opened the door and walked in.

The master asked, "How is everything outside?"
"It is all dark."
"Anything else?"
"Nothing at all."
"No," said the master, "Outside is fresh wind, green fields, flowers and plants, brooks ... everything is still there."

21. The Master's Smile

A monk joyously approached the Master Wei Chueh in his office to report his meditation experience. The Master looked at him, smiled, and did not say anything. After a few days, this monk was annoyed by something, so he came again to the Master to complain about his difficulty. The Master still looked at him and smiled without saying a word.

Looking at the Master's familiar smile, this monk thought about the distinctly different state of mind that he was in a few days ago. The Master's smile reminded him of the Buddha's teaching, "To be calm in quietness is not true stillness; to be calm in chaos is true stillness."

22. Doubt

A monk said to Zen Master Yaoshan, "I have doubt. I ask the master to resolve it for me."

Yaoshan said, "Wait until I go into the hall tonight to speak. Then I'll resolve it."

That evening, Yaoshan entered the hall. When the assembly was ready, he said, "Where is the monk who asked me today to resolve his doubt?"

The monk came forward and stood there.

Yaoshan got down from the Dharma seat, grabbed the monk, and said, "Everyone! This monk has doubt!"

Yaoshan then released the monk and went back to his room.

23. Solution

Once a monk asked Zen Master Yaoshan, "How can I avoid being confused by all kinds of outside appearances?"

The master said, "Just leave them alone and they won't bother you."

The monk was unsatisfied with this. The master asked, "What 'outside appearances' are confusing you right now?"

24. Any Question

Zen master Rinzai once said:
"Does anyone have a question? If so, let him ask it now. But the instant you open your mouth you are already way off. "

25. Sign

A monk asked Dasui, "What is the sign of a great man?"
Dasui said, "He doesn't have a placard on his stomach."

26. Miracle

Zen master Keui-shan was taking a nap one day when Yang-shan came and greeted him. Keui-shan turned sleepily to the wall. Yang-shan asked, "Why did you do that?"

"I just had a dream," Keui-shan replied, "Can you interpret it for me?"

Yang-shan left the room, returning a few moments later with a basin of cold water for his teacher's face. Soon Hsiang-yen also came to greet his teacher, whereat Keui-shan said, "Your brother monk has just interpreted my dream. What is your interpretation?"

Hsiang-yen went out quietly and returned with a cup of tea for his teacher. Keui-shan commented, "You two monks perform miracles."

27. The Last Rap

Tangen had studied with Sengai since childhood. When he was twenty he wanted to leave his teacher, and visit others for comparative study, but Sengai would not permit this. Every time Tangen suggested it, Sengai would give him a rap on the head.

Finally, Tangen asked an elder brother to coax permission from Sengai. This the brother did and then reported to Tangen: "It is arranged. I have fixed it for you start your pilgrimage at once."

Tangen went to Sengai to thank him for his permission. The master answered by giving him another rap.

When Tangen related this to his elder brother the other said: "What is the matter? Sengai has no business giving permission and then changing his mind. I will tell him so." And off he went to see the teacher.

"I did not cancel my permission," said Sengai. "I just wished to give him one last smack over the head, for when he returns he will be enlightened and I will not be able to reprimand him again."

28. Who Are Buddhas?

A monk asked Zen Master Luzu Baoyun of Chizhou, "Who are all the Buddhas and saints?"

Baoyun said, "Not the ones with crowns on their heads."

The monk said, "Then who are they?"

Baoyun said, "The ones without crowns."

29. Half Approve, Half Not Approve

Zen Master Dongshan hosted a feast of commemoration on the anniversary of his master Yunyan's death.

A monk asked, "When you were at Yunyan's place, what teaching did he give you?"

Dongshan said, "Although I was there, I didn't receive any teaching."

The monk asked, "But you are holding a commemorative feast for the late teacher. Doesn't that show you approve his teaching?"

Dongshan said, "Half approve. Half not approve."

The monk said, "Why don't you completely approve of it?"

Dongshan said, "If I completely approved, then I would be disloyal to my late teacher."

30. The Complete Entrance

A monk said, "I've just arrived at the monastery. I ask the master to reveal to me the complete entrance."

Zen Master Baofu said, "If I were to show you the complete entrance, then I would just bow to you."

31. Donkey

Zen Master Foyan said, "I say there are but two types of sickness. One is to ride a donkey to look for a donkey. The other is riding a donkey and not let yourself get off of it. Don't you see that riding a donkey to find a donkey is a fatal disease? This old mountain monk is telling you, don't seek it! Clever people understand right where they are. They give up the 'seeking' disease and the crazy, thought pursuing mind. Once you've seen the donkey, not allowing yourself to get off it - now that is a disease that is most hard to cure. This old mountain monk is telling you, don't ride it!

"You are the donkey! The great Earth is the donkey! How are you going to ride it? If you continue to ride it you'll never cure this disease. If you don't ride it then all the worlds in the ten directions are opened to you. If you can get rid of both of these diseases at once, then there's nothing left in your mind, and you are called a person of the way. What could trouble you?

"Therefore, Zhaozhou asked Nanquan, 'What is the way?' and Nanquan answered, 'Everyday mind is the way'."

32. Illness

When Zen Master Dongshan Liangjie was not feeling well, a monastic said, "Master, you are not feeling well. Is there anyone who doesn't get sick?"

Dongshan said, "Yes, there is."

The monastic said, "Does the person who doesn't get sick take care of you?"

Dongshan said, "I have the opportunity to take care of the person."

The monastic said, "What happens when you take care of that person?"

Dongshan said, "At that time, I don't see the sickness."

33. The Question

Said the monk, "All these mountains and rivers and earth and stars — where do they come from?"
Said the Master, "Where does your question come from?"
Search within!

34. Perception

Dear Friends, let me tell you a little story a wise man once told me. He said: "Once I found myself in an unfamiliar country, walking down a strange street. I looked around trying to get my bearings; and seeing two men who were standing nearby, I approached them. `Where am I?' I asked. `Who are you people?'
"The first man replied, `This is the world of Samsara, and in this world, I happen to be the very tallest dwarf there is!' And the other man replied, `Yes, and I happen to be the shortest giant!'
"This encounter left me very confused because, you see, both men were exactly the same height."
I preface my remarks to you with this little story because I want to emphasize at the outset how important it is to consider the perception of things. [...]
In the world of Samsara, Man is the measure of all things. Everything is relative. Everything is changing. Only in the real world, the world of Nirvana, is there constancy.

~ Zen Master Xu Yun ~

35. Tradition

Someone asked: "What is your tradition?"
The Zen master said: "Not choosing food when hungry."

36. The Buddha In The Home

One day, a young man named Yang fu left his parents to go to Sichuan (Szechwan) to visit the bodhisattva Wuji.

He met a Zen Master in the way who asked, "Where are you going young man?" "

Yang Fu said, "I am going to study under Wuji the bodhisattva."

"Instead of looking for a mere bodhisattva, you'd be better off looking for the Buddha."

"Do you know where I can find the Buddha?"

"When you return home, a person wearing a blanket and with shoes on the wrong feet will come to greet you. That person is the Buddha."

"Really?"

Yang fu hurried back. Arriving at his home late at night. In her joyful haste to greet her returning son Yang fu's mother three on a blanket and accidentally put her slippers on the wrong feet. Yang fu took one look at her and was suddenly enlightened.

37. Monkey's Response

Yangshan once asked the Zen Master Hongen:
"How can I have the experience of seeing my own nature?"
"It's like small house with six open windows and a baby monkey inside. If a person calls the monkey from the east side, when the monkey responds, the sound will come from all six windows."

38. Understanding

A monk asked, "If someone is seeking an understanding of Buddha, what's the best path to doing so?"
Zen Master Fayan Wenyi (885-958) said, "It doesn't pass here."

39. Archery

A Zen Master observing students at archery practice notices one of them who is consistently missing the mark, and says: "It is his desire to win that drains him of power."

40. People

There was a person coming to a new village, relocating, and he was wondering if he would like it there, so he went to a zen master and asked: Do you think I will like it in this village? Are the people nice? The master asked back: How were the people on the town where you come from? "They were nasty and greedy, they were angry and lived for cheating and stealing," said the newcomer.

"Those are exactly the type of people we have in this village," said the master.

Another newcomer to the village visited the master and asked the same question, to which the master asked: How were the people in the town where you come from? "They were sweet and lived in harmony, they cared for one another and for the land, they respected each other and they were seekers of spirit," he replied.

"Those are exactly the type of people we have in this village," said the master!

41. The Painting

Once upon a time there was a Shogun who wanted a nice picture of a chicken to go in his tokonoma.
So, he went to a very fine artist (Hiroshige? Sharaku?) and said, "I want you to paint me the best picture of a chicken that you can."
So, the artist said, "Hai, hai, mochiron, kore o shimasu." (Yes, yes, certainly, I will do this.)
The artist went to his cabin high on Mount Fuji. He brought books of bird anatomy, many studies of birds done by all the famous artists of the past, He sculpted chickens, he painted chickens in oil, he did one woodblock after another of nothing but chickens. He depicted chickens in bushido poses, crashing through the shoji in a samurai palace. He drew noble portraits of chickens in virtuous attitudes. He used a sumie brush to catch every nuance of a chicken's life. He painted chickens in the landscape and in the boudoir, on the battlefield and in the barn.
Ten years passed.

One day the shogun was at archery practice when he thought of his request to the artist. He immediately mounted his steed and made his way to the artist's cabin. It was hard to enter the door. There were sketches of chickens stacked to the ceiling. There were statues of chickens everywhere. There were skeletons of chickens and paintings of chickens. There was nowhere to sit and very little space to stand.
"Where is my chicken drawing?" demanded the Shogun.
"Oh," said the artist, "I forgot, sorry." And he took a brush, whirled it very quickly on a piece of rice paper, handed the paper to the Shogun, and said, "Here."

42. Let Go

A man visited a great mystic to find out how to let go of his chains of attachment and his prejudices. Instead of answering him directly, the mystic jumped to his feet and bolted to a nearby pillar, flung his arms around it, grasping the marble surface as he screamed, "Save me from this pillar! Save me from this pillar!"

The man who had asked the question could not believe what he saw. He thought the mystic was mad. The shouting soon brought a crowd of people. "Why are you doing that?" the man asked. "I came to you to ask a spiritual question because I thought you were wise, but obviously, you're crazy. You are holding the pillar; the pillar is not holding you. You can simply let go."

The mystic let go of the pillar and said to the man, "If you can understand that, you have your answer. Your chains of attachment are not holding you, you are holding them. You can simply let go."

43. Emotion

A Zen story concerns an elder monk in a Japanese monastery. The young novices were in awe of this man, not because he was severe with them, but because nothing ever seemed to upset him. A few of the young men decided to test the monk by devising a plan to scare him.

Early one dark winter morning, it was the monk's duty to carry tea to the Founders Hall. The young men hid in the alcove of a long and winding corridor near the entrance to the hall. Just as the monk passed, they rushed out screaming like crazy men. Without faltering a step, the monk continued walking on quietly, carefully carrying the tea. When he arrived at his destination he set down the tray, covered the tea bowl so no dust could fall into it and then fell back against the wall and cried out in shock "Oh-oh-oh!"

A Zen Master relating this story said, "There is nothing wrong with emotions. Only one must not let them carry one away, or interfere with what one is doing."

44. The Mind

A Zen story tells of two monks who met on the road. After their initial greetings, one monk asked the other, "What are you going to do tonight, my friend?" The second monk replied, "I will meditate and pray in the temple. What are you going to do?" "I'm going to spend a night of pleasure with the ladies," he answered.

The monks then went on their own ways, and that night in the house of pleasure, the monk was quite distracted. All he could think about was his friend meditating and praying. But was the other monk at peace with himself? No, he continued to think about his friend enjoying an evening with women.

When you make a choice, accept it completely and surrender to all the experiences that go along with your decision.

45. The True Self

A distraught man approached the Zen master. "Please, Master, I feel lost, desperate. I don't know who I am. Please, show me my true self!" But the teacher just looked away without responding. The man began to plead and beg, but still the master gave no reply. Finally giving up in frustration, the man turned to leave. At that moment, the master called out to him by name. "Yes!" the man said as he spun back around. "There it is!" exclaimed the master.

46. Imitation

A disciple who loved and admired his Zen teacher decided to observe his behavior minutely, believing that if he did everything that his teacher did, then he would also acquire his teacher's wisdom. The teacher always wore white, and so his disciple did the same. The teacher was a vegetarian, and so his disciple stopped eating meat and replaced it with a diet of vegetables and herbs. The teacher was an austere man, and so the disciple decided to devote himself to self-sacrifice and started sleeping on a straw mattress.

After some time, the teacher noticed these changes in his disciple's behavior and asked him why.

'I am climbing the steps of initiation,' came the reply.

'The white of my clothes shows the simplicity of my search, the vegetarian food purifies my body, and the lack of comfort makes me think only of spiritual things.'

Smiling, the teacher took him to a field where a horse was grazing.

'You have spent all this time looking outside yourself, which is what matters least,' he said. 'Do you see that creature there? He has white skin, eats only grass and sleeps in a stable on a straw bed. Do you think he has the face of a saint or will one day become a real teacher?'

47. The Strange Advice

A novice once went to a Zen Master to ask his advice on how best to become enlightened. 'Go to the cemetery and insult the dead,' said the master.

The brother did as he was told. The following day, he went back to the master. 'Did they respond?' asked the master.

'No,' said the novice.

'Then go and praise them instead.'

The novice obeyed. That same afternoon, he went back to the master, who again asked if the dead had responded.

'No, they didn't,' said the novice.

'In order to become enlightened, do exactly as they did,' master told him.

'Take no notice of men's scorn or of their praise; in that way, you will be able to build your own path.

48. Fees

A Zen Master spent his whole life teaching that all the answers to our questions are in ourselves, but his congregation insisted on consulting him about everything they did.

One day, the master had an idea. He placed a notice on the door of his house, saying: 'ANSWERS TO QUESTIONS – 1000 YEN PER ANSWER.'

A shopkeeper decided to pay the one thousand yens. He gave the rabbi the money and said: 'Don't you think that's rather a lot to charge for a question?'

'Yes, I do,' said the master. 'And I have just answered your question. If you want to know anything else, you'll have to pay another one thousand yens, or else look for the answer inside yourself, which is far cheaper and much more efficient.'

From then on, no one bothered him.

49. Correct

Two monks who came out of a lecture by their master went on a hot debate regarding what they heard during the lecture. Each of them insited that his understanding was the correct one. To settle the dispute, they went to see the master for a judgement.

After hearing the argument put forth by the first monk, the master said, "You are correct!" The monk was overjoyed. Casting a winner's glance at his friend, he left the room.

The second monk was upset and started to pour out what he thought to the master. After he finished, the master looked at him and said, "You are correct, too." Hearing this, the second monk brightened up and went away.

A third monk who was also in the room was greatly puzzled by what he saw. He said to the master, "I am confused, master! Their positions regarding the issue are completely opposite. They can't be both right! How could you say that they are both correct?"

The master smiled as he looked into the eyes of this third monk, "You are also correct!"

50. The Entrance To Zen

A monk was anxious to learn Zen and said, "I have been newly initiated into the Brotherhood and will you be gracious enough to show me the way to Zen?"
The master said, "Do you hear the murmuring sound of the mountain stream?"
The monk answered, "Yes, I do."
The master said, "Here is the entrance."

What Next?

Great that you finished these fifty stories. What next?

The Zen Masters are the people who have spent a lot of time in meditation. Then only they preach others. If you just read the stories and do not meditate at all, you will miss the whole point. Go to different meditation centers. Try few meditation techniques and then find the one which suits you most. After a few months of practice, when you will read these same zen stories, you will find many hidden meanings.

These stories are not something which you read once and forget. These stories carry the most pregnant wisdom available on earth. Work hard on meditation and revisit this story again after some time. Perhaps then you will understand what I am pointing to!

Bibliography

1. Zen's Chinese Heritage by Andy Ferguson
2. Treasury of the Forest of Ancestors by Satyavayu
3. Zen Flesh, Zen Bones
4. Recorded Sayings of Joshu
5. The Blue Cliff Record
6. Shoyoroku
7. Records of Zen Master Rinzai
8. Dogen's 300 Koans
9. Zen Koans by Kubose
10. Zen Speaks: Shouts of Nothingness by Tsai Chih Chung
11. The Original Teachings of Ch'an Buddhism by Chang Ching Yuan
12. The Golden Age of Zen by John Ching Hsiung Wu
13. I am the Dewdrop; I am the Ocean by Satish Gupta
14. Wikipedia and various other sources on internet

www.ingramcontent.com/pod-product-compliance
Lightning Source LLC
Chambersburg PA
CBHW072110290426
44110CB00014B/1883